Trailing Around Asia

Mud, Sweat & Bears

HARRIET GAYWOOD

All rights reserved. No portion of this book may be reproduced in any form without written permission from the author.

Copyright © 2025 Harriet Gaywood

All rights reserved.

ISBN: 9798345096147

To Anoushka and Mischa

In addition, I want to dedicate 'Trailing Around Asia: Mud, Sweat & Bears' to the China trail running community who have given me so much support, welcoming and encouraging me to go further, and to the wonderful volunteer led FitFam community for keeping me fit when I am not on a trail.

MUD, SWEAT & BEARS

CONTENTS

	Introduction	1
	My races in 2024	4
	Map of Race Locations	6
1	Everyman's Everest	7
2	Geckos & Jungle	11
3	Bamboo & Rice	15
4	Karst Caverns & Cuckoos	20
5	Jade Dragons & Bears	26
6	Wild Sage on the Solstice	32
7	Wildflowers and Firs	38
8	Mud or Fine Porcelain?	43
9	Bear Growls above the Clouds	47
10	The Four Sisters	52
11	Island Life on Stilts	59
12	Elephants & Gold	62
13	Kit Essentials	69
14	Nutrition	71
15	Training	72
16	Reflections the Cave	73

MUD, SWEAT & BEARS

INTRODUCTION

Before you read this, it is important to emphasize that "Trailing Around Asia: Mud, Sweat & Bears" is not a guide about how to do trail running or run faster but a collection of stories about my personal experiences running ultramarathons during 2024. At the start of the year I didn't set out on a mission to either run lots of races or write this short book but as I started to recap some of the races and places I was visiting, I thought it might be interesting to put them together to give an insight into trail running and ultramarathons in Asia, and perhaps inspire some people to understand that while winning an ultramarathon may be difficult, running, completing and enjoying such a race is quite attainable. More importantly, taking up a hobby or taking on new challenges at any age can be rewarding.

I wasn't a runner previously and sometimes still hesitate to call myself one. I was focused on my career and lived in a blur between building businesses in China's fast-developing economy and all-consuming work environment and balancing family life on the other. I was always running but usually between clients, schools and whatever weekend activity was happening. I certainly wasn't lacing up my trail shoes. But at some point, one's health becomes important. And so, it happened. One day at work we decided to run a charity 5k as a team. I agreed but inwardly was panicking – I wasn't sure I would be able to run so far.

This was perhaps the kick I needed. Already in my early forties, I gradually started running on the streets of Shanghai and signed up for increasingly longer distances to eventually run a marathon. I still remember the excitement of running into Shanghai Stadium together with 35,000 other runners at the end of the race. But it wasn't until I completed my first trail race when I realized the difference between running on tarmac and the endless possibilities of a trail – climbing up hills to see views across tea plantations and descending through trees on steep earthen paths. This experience of running trails compared with paved roads, combined with a post-Covid daily desire to be close to greenery cemented my love of trail races, and in particular ultra marathons, which refers to races over 50k.

For those of you who aren't familiar with trail racing, courses tend to pass along a mix of public and private hillside paths, villages, paved roads and tracks marked by reflective ribbons which are visible during the day and catch the beam of a headtorch at night. In general, the courses follow a circular shape or a figure of eight and will finish in the same place that they begin but there are also exceptions with A to B routes. On average checkpoints are placed every 10k allowing runners to refuel their water and drinks, take on food and nutrition, and obtain first aid if needed. The location of these refreshment stations is usually determined by road access although there are exceptions (see Chapter 10: The Four Sisters).

Not all the races I ran this year are covered in this book, but I chose the places and experiences that I felt were most interesting. I also did races in Wugongshan, Jiangxi and Lingshan near Beijing all of which offered long climbs up winding paths, transformed into velvety green pastures in the summer after becoming dry and desolate during the winter.

I am not well-placed to give counsel to others in terms of running advice except to say that training does pay off. There are many incredible runners and coaches who can provide training plans, nutrition suggestions and all sorts of other advice regarding trail running both online and offline.

As I write this introduction I am flying over the now ice and snow covered sandy yet barren mountains just south of Jiuquan, Gansu Province, China in the Gobi Desert where I ran my first 100k race several years ago. It is a reminder of the beauty of the earth and how vulnerable we are to the elements whether in the vastness of the dry, cold desert or in the tropical storms on the mountainside. It is experiencing these extremes that inspires me to go further. It is also a reminder that as runners we always have to respect the environment.

I am fortunate to have done some incredible journeys this year and hopefully this book might inspire you to either visit some of these places or at least put on your shoes and find some greenery nearby to enjoy!

Notes:

Brand Mentions

I am not sponsored by any brands and pay all my own costs such as race entry and travel costs so any brand mentions are incidental or simply reflect the event sponsor or official name of the race.

Many of the races are part of the UTMB® World Series. UTMB stands for Ultra-Trail du Mont-Blanc, one of the toughest ultramarathons in the world which starts in Courmayeur. The route winds through Italy, Switzerland and France with a finish in Chamonix, France. Inaugurated in 2003 it is one of the key trail races of the year. UTMB has now become a recognized brand lending its name to races all over the world as part of the UTMB® World Series.

Photography credits

Unless otherwise stated, all photos and copyright belong to the author and may not be reproduced without express permission.

Measurement

In trail running there are lots of discrepancies in terms of measuring height and distance. This is because paths winding on hills are simply hard to measure. It is further complicated by race categories which typically designated as 50k, 100k and 100miles but may not reflect the exact distance. The race list below states the official name of the race. For example, Trans-Int 160 in Chiang Mai was actually 172k.

MY RACES IN 2024

Guangzhou 100 Ultra Trail Race 2024 – 100k-GZ100, Guangdong Province, China

The Ultra-Trail Huangshan Xihong Spring 168 2024, Huangshan, Anhui Province, China

Mount Yun by UTMB 2024 – DMY 100k, Shanxi Province, China

Amazean Jungle Thailand by UTMB 2024, Betong 100, Yala Province, Thailand

Shangrao Lingshan 100 Ultra Trail Race, Shangrao, Jiangxi Province, China

2024 The 12th Tiankeng Capital International Mountain Cross Country Race & China100 Mountain Cross Country Series (China-Leye), Guangxi Province, China

YL Extreme Cross Country Race 100k, Jade Snow Dragon Mountain Lijiang, Yunnan Province, China

MY RACES IN 2024 (continued)

Chicheng Ultra Trail – CTT 168k, Chicheng, Hebei Proince, China

Adidas TERREX Chongli 168 Ultra Trail 2024 - UTC, Hebei Province, China

Wugong Shan 56, Jiangxi Province, China

Kailas Ultra Tour Mt. Siguniang MHZL75, Sichuan Province, China

Anta Guanjun Gaoligong Ultra MGU 168, Tengchong, Yunnan Province, China

Ultra-Trail Ninghai by UTMB 2024 - UTNH105, Zhejiang Province, China

TransLantau by UTMB 2024 TranLantau 120, Hong Kong, China

UTMB Asia Pacific Major Trans-Int 160, Chiang Mai, Thailand

The North Face Hong Kong 100, Hong Kong, China

MAP OF RACE LOCATIONS

Source: Google Maps

Trailing Around Asia Map.

- Betong
- Chiangmai
- Chicheng
- Chongli
- Hong Kong
- Lijiang
- Leye
- Ninghai
- Siguniang
- Shangrao
- Tengchong

1 EVERYMAN'S EVEREST

"Well, IF you were an athlete, your heart might be this rate" the local town doctor said as he looked at me in slight disbelief and approved my health-check ahead of an ultra-marathon in a remote part of China. "IF you are a runner, where is your team?" a lady asked me on a bus as I travelled to another race. I often ask myself the same question. Am I an athlete or a runner or just somebody in midlife trying to stay fit?

In a year where I ran over 1,850 km of races and climbed over 90,000m (the equivalent of over ten times the height of Mount Everest) including seven 100k races and six 168k (100 mile) races, I still remain in awe of the title 'athlete', but having reached half a century in age, I know I am lucky to be able to run and also that I can do more. Of course, this isn't the same as climbing Mount Everest which requires a lot more skill and support. But sharing the height climbed gives you an idea of the difference between road running and trail running.

This year I challenged myself to run races in a variety of terrains, temperatures and altitudes. Most races have a distinguishing feature – whether the course, landmarks or even the local cuisine. For example, I kicked off the year with the Guangzhou 100. Although the route was impressive for its steep hills and surprisingly green given its proximity to a city of 18 million people, it was most memorable for its emphasis on food. There were food stations nearly every five kilometres with local dumplings and Cantonese dim sum so it was more of a gastronomic experience rather than a race and I certainly didn't go hungry. Eating dim sum may not be part of every race, but nutrition and eating well is critical so the topic is covered later in this book.

During the year I have run in temperatures ranging from the mid-thirties Celsius down to minus 10. I experienced weather conditions from strong sun and blue skies to heavy rain, ice, snow, high winds and mist. Wet weather and the consequent slippery and muddy conditions created underfoot affect decisions about clothing which in turn affects speed, hydration and hunger.

Running at altitude requires planning. 'High altitude' is between 1,500 to 3,500m and 'very high altitude' is from 3,500 to 5,500. My races included three 'high altitude' and three 'very high altitude' courses. For very high altitude, acclimatization is essential. This means arriving a few days before the race, resting and getting used to thinner air. I learned not to have a hot shower on the first day of arriving in altitude to prevent blood moving away from my heart which can cause fainting and to always wear a cap or hat to keep the sun off my head.

With higher altitude comes greater unpredictability in the weather. Very hot sun can turn to cold torrential rain in just a few minutes. So I have included a kit list at the end of the book for reference. Typically refreshments are provided every 10k so water bottles can be refilled with either hot or cold water together with snacks such as a banana, nuts or fruit. Some checkpoints offer more substantial food such as noodles, rice, and congee.

For 100k races, we are allowed to have a 'drop bag' which can be accessed at a checkpoint around halfway for changing clothes, shoes, and resupplying nutrition. For 168k races there will usually be two opportunities to change. Nevertheless, for longer distances, our backpacks will still be slightly heavier due to carrying more supplies. In addition to carrying a compulsory waterproof, emergency blanket, whistle, headtorch and food, we will also carry a supplementary headtorch, and clothes for nighttime when the air is damp and colder. Failure to carry compulsory items can result in time penalties or even race disqualification. Apart from the obvious advantage of carrying less weight and therefore being able to run faster, penalties is intended to reinforce the importance of safety.

During trail runs close encounters with animals are frequent and generally harmless. Grumpy wild boar and pigs are common. At higher altitude we share the paths with wild ponies, cattle, goats and yaks and generally they assume right of way. The title of this book mentions bears which were nearby on three races. I had one close encounter with a bear in Yunnan Province which was just a few meters away. In Siguniang, late at night in the dark, I saw a warning sign about bears nearby. The winner of the 100k race did see one but thankfully it had gone when I came through! In the jungles of Thailand, leeches present the biggest danger so long socks aren't just to support muscles but to keep creepy crawlies off the skin.

In Asia, the trails are usually not just on public paths but laid out by people with a deep knowledge of the local area creating routes that traverse forgotten stone paths, bamboo forests, tea plantations, farm steadings and temples and which rely on the goodwill of local villagers and farmers. It is often these same local people who provide incredible smiling hospitality, serving food at checkpoints and making sure everybody is looked after before heading off, often in the darkness, to the next checkpoint.

They say travel is about the journey not the destination and this is often true of actually getting to races in Asia. In China the high-speed trains have transformed domestic travel and whilst competition for tickets can be fierce at weekends, the trains travel an average of 300-350k per hour making it quite feasible to travel long distances without the hassle of taking a plane. However, some of the plane journeys have also been fun. In Baise a remote town in Guangxi Province, the small plane from Shenzhen simply landed on the runway and allowed a few of us to disembark before continuing on to Kunming in Yunnan Province. The tiny luggage conveyor could only hold about five items. During a separate journey to Tengchong via Kunming, the transfer desks were handling transfers for 31 regional airlines that only fly within Southwest China.

I generally try to be travel neutral and opt for the quickest or most reliable option whether bus, moped, plane, taxi or train. Sharing taxis is a common business model for taxi drivers in the countryside which can result in fun encounters and conversations. Accommodation can also be variable with price not necessarily being an indicator of quality. Chinese trains, bus stations, railway stations and airports always provide hot water, so travel is generally quite comfortable even on a long journey with a water bottle and some tea! Until recently foreigners in China were restricted in terms of the hotels that they were allowed to stay in. Late in 2024 the policy changed but smaller hotels are often unaware of this. Usually, I simply try to stay as close as possible to the start line of a race so that I don't have too far to go at the end of a gruelling race.

2 GECKOS & JUNGLE

80% humidity, 33 degrees Celsius in the sun, muddy and slippery underfoot, steep climbs through the undergrowth, over 12 hours in darkness with a headtorch, 30 hours in total!

It is 4am when we set off for the Amazean Trail 2024 part of the UTMB World Series. We are in Betong, a small low-rise town on the Thai-Malay border with traditional wooden-fronted houses and shops. We set off along the quiet streets and soon turn onto a track which in turn becomes a narrow path uphill. The first climb of the 6240m total elevation begins. With a mix of fast walking and running we reach the first checkpoint at 10km most people have already fallen at least once on the steep muddy slopes which are wet after heavy rain the day before.

Daylight is just breaking as we cross a main road and carry on up into the jungle. As we follow the undulating valleys it is hard to tell if we are actually climbing to higher ground. But the trees change, an indication that we are indeed getting higher. Below our feet the paths become steeper with tree roots and earth sometimes covered with a thick carpet of tropical leaves. Some of the plants are giant with leaves bigger than any I have seen before. Enormous trees regularly block the way dotted with the most beautiful coloured fungi and moss. The sound of waterfalls flowing over rocks and a quick face splash and hand wash in the cool water of the pools below them is both mentally and physically refreshing.

Eventually we reach a summit and find ourselves above the clouds staring down at thick greenery with occasional trees shooting above the forest.

It is the noise of the jungle that amazes me the most — I hear geckos and cuckoos plus a myriad of insects. It is night. I am alone with my headtorch following reflective markers that catch its beam but I never feel afraid in the company of the forest despite the remoteness. However I do worry about whether any leeches have latched onto me in the darkness.

The author in the jungle near Betong, Thailand. Credit: Running Connect

From running, jogging, walking, climbing to eating, drinking and sleeping. Survival is about hydration — every 10k I fill up with another 1 liter of water and sip a few glasses of water and hydration drinks. I grab a few snacks or a bowl of rice. The climbing and the heat sap my energy. Rest or keep going? This is the ongoing question that consumes me at every checkpoint. This time I opt for rest because these conditions are unknown to me but never rest for too long because I don't know what is ahead, and how long a section might take to complete.

Blisters, dehydration, sprains, fatigue. At every rest station I see people who are exhausted or injured. They make assessments based on their own experience and the advice of medical teams about whether or not to continue.

Eventually we are at the 80k point — this is also a critical juncture of the race because mentally time is getting tight. As I walk out of the checkpoint I know that I haven't had enough of a rest and I am hungry — but I am also slightly behind in the race and need to make up time.

Competition rules stipulate that you must leave the checkpoint before it closes so I head out into the darkness and into the quiet streets of a village. I sit by the roadside and shut my eyes for a few moments. The tiredness has kicked in and my sleep is instant but short-lived. A couple of minutes later I am moving again. I walk a couple of kilometres. But the same tiredness kicks in again. I sit among the plants at the side of the road. A couple of other runners come past. I allow myself to drop into sleep for a couple of minutes then awake with a jolt. I pick myself up and move again.

I keep sipping water and finally I push through my tiredness. Daylight is breaking again. As the sun slowly rises piercing the mist in the valleys of rubber trees and banana palms, the beauty of the wildflowers and the light flickering though the leaves lead me along a red clay track. My energy returns — where I was wavering, I now feel revived. There is a sign for the penultimate checkpoint at a temple. I stride up a steep paved road to the top of a hill but can't see the temple. Although it is still early the sun is already strong and feels scorching on my skin. The road winds down the hill again. I feel slightly deflated about not finding the promised temple but run down the hill and find the checkpoint looking out across the hills. I grab some water, leave the road and start running down narrow winding earth paths.

Down and down the hill then past vegetable patches. Suddenly we are on another road, heading back into Betong. Small children have set up a hose and fill up cups of water to wash our hands. People offer cups of iced drinking water along the road while others cheer from restaurants. The town, so quiet 30 hours before at the 3am start, is now alive and buzzing with excitement. People line the streets shouting encouragement. Soldiers are holding back the traffic and waving me on. I cross the finish line in a state of shock, exhaustion and euphoria!

79 out of the original 181 runners complete the course. At 67th I am one of the last people to finish the course and the 16th woman overall. After collecting a wooden medal and a trophy made of local porcelain for coming second place in my age category I head back to my hotel. I shower and lie down to sleep for an hour then wake up in panic after oversleeping. I am supposed to be catching one of only two daily minibuses heading north out of Betong.

I hastily checkout from my hotel. My taxi driver assumes I am heading to Malaysia rather than Had Yai in Thailand, and speeds towards the international bus station. Realising we are driving out of town I frantically bang on the cab window from the open jeepney. The driver stops in the middle of the highway, flags down a tuktuk and I hop in and we speed to the correct bus station. I have no idea what happened during the conversation between the two drivers, but I arrive on the forecourt of the bus station deserted except for my bus with just one minute to spare I find my seat and finally can fall asleep as we wind our way down the mountain on a hot Sunday afternoon. Four hours later I wake up as we arrive back in the bustling town of Had Yai in Southern Thailand.

3 BAMBOO & RICE

Every race in China is an adventure. Since races are in the countryside this often means traveling to small towns, then onwards to a national park or scenic area. I travel to Lingshan, a scenic mountain area near Shangrao, a small town in Jiangxi Province, China — 500k and about three hours travel by high-speed train from Shanghai. Reaching speeds of up to 380k an hour, these trains and their impressive new railway network have made it possible to attend races in places that were previously inaccessible or simply too far away for a weekend jaunt.

The Shangrao Lingshan 100 Ultra Trail is in a stunning spot — the mountain range looms above the race start cutting a jagged outline against the sky. I stay in a local guesthouse. It is basic but within walking distance to the race start. In China it is sometimes difficult to find taxis in the countryside, especially early in the morning so I always try to stay close to the race area. Waking at 4am I have breakfast (chia porridge and coffee — I always need caffeine and bring my own supplies). At 5am I head to the start line with my race bag and drop bag (for use at Checkpoint 6 out of the total 10).

Shanghai where I live is flat so I always enjoy getting to the hills. Race routes in China typically cut through rice paddies, tea plantations and bamboo forests. The terrain can be tracks, ancient trading paths with broken stone steps or simply fresh routes following ribbons through the forest. There is usually a segment on paved road.

View from Lingshan, Jiangxi Province, China

We start off at 6am after singing the Chinese national anthem, some warmup exercises and a start gun fired by some local government officials. The 100k and 50k race start together and head up the road (the 30k group start an hour later). After a couple of kilometres, we turn off and start on an ancient route climbing steeply through the forest. We start at 170m above sea level and at 1,046m we reach the first checkpoint, refill our water and grab snacks. We continue to the summit at 1,386m and follow a winding concrete ledge that has been added to the side of the mountain. The guardrails are designed to imitate curving branches. I have a slight fear of slipping off the side so I take it slowly as we contour around the top of the mountain.

Just two hours into the race, the sun is getting strong. I have a cap, sunglasses, sunblock, arm sleeves and I am consciously drinking water every few minutes to ensure I don't become dehydrated. Gatorade is served at the checkpoints and I find myself unusually drawn to it. At every race I find myself sticking to one particular drink. During one winter race

I drank the malted Ovaltine and at another, seaweed soup. Sweet ginger tea is another favourite.

It is getting warm but there are cold streams bubbling down the mountain. Like many of the runners I stop to wash my face and hands to cool down. While the top of the mountain is exposed rock, the descent down the mountain is in the shade. I pass two more checkpoints and then start a particularly steep climb. The sunlight is reaching through the foliage and it feels hot. Runners rest in the shade then carry on uphill in a steady, determined way. I stick to the shadows and enjoy the beauty of the trees and bamboo towering above me as I climb up treading over a mix of ancient stones, soft earth and leaves.

It feels tough and although I am tempted to rest I keep going using my running poles to propel myself uphill. At the top of the mountain there is a small stone gateway which provides cover. Like a couple of other runners, I sit down for a moment to recover from the climb then run down the other side of the mountain to the next checkpoint. I am slow going uphill but faster going downhill in contrast to many of the other runners (especially some of the locals who seem to breeze effortlessly over the hills).

I get to the next checkpoint. I refill my water again and grab some more snacks ready to move on, but a lady stops me. They have just been informed that the race has been suspended due to the heat. It is hotter than I thought — 35 degrees Celsius! All of the runners have to wait for more updates then we are told to return to the start point.

We are in a small village. A small shop does a roaring trade in ice cream and cold water as we wait and exchange race stories. A bus is sent to pick us up but it can't drive up the road due to low overhead cables so we walk in the hot sun through fields for a couple of km and eventually spot our transport.

8 hours in. We have only covered 32km and climbed 2,400m. The hardest parts of the race have been completed but the danger of the unexpected heat is real over a long race. Some of the runners are suffering and the

risk is too high. By coincidence it is exactly three years since China lost 20 trail runners in a devastating freak weather accident, so the organisers are conscious of the risks and safety is paramount.

Rice terraces near Lingshan, Jiangxi Province, China

35 degrees Celsius can feel hot especially in direct sun. Medical care in China is improving but most small villages and third-tier cities lack the facilities to cope with a sudden influx of casualties — especially trail runners. Did I want to continue my race? Of course I did but trail racing in China is fast-growing and it is essential that it is safe and well-managed to prevent avoidable incidents otherwise nobody will want to host races. The hills will always be there.

Feeling slightly deflated I head back to my guesthouse. There aren't any guesthouses here that accept foreigners, but the manager has let me stay on the basis that I just need a room. My guesthouse doesn't serve food so I wander down the road and find one that does. Mealtimes are strict because serving food is to provide supplementary income for the local farmers who are busy working in the fields as their main work. Unusually for China, dinner doesn't start until after 7pm but when it arrives, the steaming plate of bamboo shoots is worth waiting for!

By the time I head back to my guesthouse past fields of vegetables, the small shop in the village that sells noodles, peanuts, pickles and water has closed and the villagers have brought out their little wooden stools to sit in the cool evening air and gossip.

4 KARST CAVERNS & CUCKOOS

Leye in Guangxi Province, Southwest China is one of the remoter towns in China — I fly from Shenzhen to the tiny airport of Baise. Arriving at midnight there are only three of us catching the 50k bus to the town. The chatty bus driver warns me that when we reach town, I should take a taxi from the bus station to my hotel even though it is close by – this surprises me as China is generally pretty safe. In the end however, when the other two passengers get off the bus, he simply drives me to the forecourt of the hotel explaining it wouldn't be possible to do this during the day! The next day I take another two-hour bus to Leye for the China 100 Leye Karst Cave International Trail running Race.

Leye is very lushly green and the landscape is covered in velvety karst lime hills. There are 11 minority groups living in this area who maintain a traditional lifestyle. In the traditional Chinese way, babies are strapped to the backs of grandmothers wearing embroidered jackets. Fruit and Chinese medicine are sold on the streets. I go for a walk to sort out my return bus ticket – I can't buy this online because only Chinese ID card holders can do this. I climb up a hill for a panorama of the town. It is hot during the day so I balance conserving my energy for the race with stretching my legs.

Waking at 4am I have breakfast, put on lots of sunblock and head to the start line for 6am. It starts raining — just enough to be refreshing as we run through small villages.

Velvety karst lime hills and maize above Leye, Guangxi Province, China

After a few kilometers we descend into a dark karst cave. It is pitch black - headtorches are essential. This race includes over 9k actually inside karst caves. These aren't just caves but huge cathedral-like caverns. There are underground pools. In some parts of the caves there are manmade paths, in others we are scrambling across slippery rocks beneath the stalactites. At some points we must lie on the ground to crawl through tiny holes in the rocks or climb up narrow shafts and pull ourselves up using our full bodyweight.

The caves are cool and damp. The climbs out of the caves are steep and the air outside feels incredibly warm and humid. By late morning the sun is getting hot. Except for one well-maintained tourist area, the route is a mix of disused, overgrown, rocky paths and tracks through forests. Stubborn ponies block the narrow path at one point and require some persuasion to let us pass.

Looking out of a sinkhole, Leye, Guangxi Province, China. Credit: China 100

By late afternoon the buzz of insects in the trees has reached a crescendo and I keep hearing cuckoo calls above the hubbub. Although the total elevation is only 3,500m in some ways it feels more because the heat is oppressive. At checkpoint 5 I take a 15-minute nap and feel refreshed but some people are feeling sick from the direct sun. I keep going. Psychologically once you have passed halfway you know you will finish.

Nevertheless, by checkpoint 7 I know I haven't eaten enough — food has been sparse on this race, and I feel slightly weak. I grab my foil blanket and lie down for a few minutes. Although it isn't cold I start shivering. I need to regulate my pace. By now it is dark. It is 10km to the next checkpoint. I walk so that I don't upset my stomach and because there is heavy dew on the paths which makes them slippery. It is misty so visibility is low.

Looking out from a karst cave, Leye, Guangxi Province Credit: China 100

As I arrive at the next checkpoint the heavens open and torrential rain starts. I put on my waterproof rain jacket and head out into the darkness. The rain looks like dash lines against the beam of my headtorch. I balance running with skipping and slipping over the wet, slippery rocks. The rain is getting heavier and in some parts I wade through deep puddles making my shoes heavy. I pass some other runners who are looking slightly bedraggled and dejected but also determined to finish. As runners, we all have different rhythms and strengths whether climbing, running or overall strength but the rain is testing everybody.

At the final checkpoint, I take a wrong turning assuming that we are heading directly back into town. I backtrack and find the trail of race marker ribbons in a quiet village with a couple of dogs barking. I see an arrow and follow it. In the dark, splashing through the puddles I cross a wooden bridge and find myself in a grotto inside the dimly outlined hill in front of me. All of a sudden, the darkness changes to a colourful underground wonderland. The walkways cross steaming underground pools in caves. I am tired and this all feels so surreal in the early hours of the morning. I am transfixed by the colours but need to concentrate and follow the paths.

Running inside a karst cave near Leye, Guangxi Province, China, Credit: China 100

I emerge from this long underground cave back out into the night just a kilometer from the finish in the town. The streets are dark and drenched by the rain. I cross a very wet finish line. 11th place out of 33 women. Around a third of the runners didn't finish. My time is exactly 22 hours.

I splosh back to my hotel ready for a hot shower to warm my body. Depressingly there is no hot water but I am so tired I quickly forget. I sleep for three hours then head to the local bus station. It is still raining in the morning and the streets are flooded but a tuk-tuk appears and the driver makes sure I catch my bus back to Baise.

Inside a karst cave, Leye, Guangxi Province, China

5 JADE DRAGONS AND BEARS

The Jade Dragon Snow Mountain Extreme Race starts from Yuhu Village near Lijiang in Yunnan Province, Southwest China. Sitting at 2,700m, the surrounding mountains are the most Southern spur of the Himalayas. The climate is warm during the day and cool at night with the proximity to the mountains making it prone to sudden changes in weather.

This 101k race is split over two days. Day 1 is 52k and day 2 is 49k. Day one of the competition starts with a steep ascent to 3,800m from Yuhu. At 6am, just as it is getting light, we head up a paved road for about 2km then onto a narrow path through trees which quickly ascends above a plain looks down on fields and towards the town of Lijiang. The sun rises. Pretty white and pink rhododendron flowers dance against the greenery. I can hear my heart beating as I climb. Although I find climbing tough at this altitude, the recovery is quick — every so often I stop and just a few seconds of rest are sufficient to catch my breath and reenergize me to continue. Towards the top, the trees stop and we arrive at a plateau at 3,800m with small hardy shrubs. The cool wind is strong but welcome after the climb. We follow the race markers up over the top of the hill and down a path of grass clumps and rocks. Checkpoint 1. I make it just in time, but many people are still behind me. The cutoff time seems tight. The path turns to woodland and a wide track so I head briskly back down the hill concerned about timing. Will I be able to keep up with the required pace?

I reach checkpoint 2, refill my water bottles, and head up the next mountain. Again this climb was to 3,800m. The sun is getting warmer and altitude makes my movement slightly laboured but I keep moving. The areas between the hills are grassy and cows roam looking for shade. By checkpoint 3 I start to tag team on the route with the same runners. One from Lijiang, one from Shanghai and one from Kunming. We all have our strengths and quickly build enough camaraderie to encourage each other as one runs ahead or another climbs faster.

Southern Himalayas in Yunnan Province, China

As I get close to the finish for Day 1, the red marker ribbons seem to stop and I lose the course. I ask one of the helpers and he assures me that I should continue heading down the track. I take his advice then realise I am on the south side of Yuhu Village instead of the north - the route was updated the day before the race and I don't think he has the latest version. The day has been hot and I know the way to the finish line but only by taking a different route. I am tempted but decide to take the honest option and head back uphill to find the original course. It costs me an extra hour but I see some of the runners whom I had met earlier in the day. We have a good laugh about my mistake and head to the finish of Day 1.

Yuhu Village is a beautiful Naxi minority village. During the day it becomes busy with tourists but at night it is very quiet and dark with no street lighting. As I walk back from Day 1, I find a restaurant still serving food then head to my hotel, organize my kit for the morning, and go straight to sleep – the altitude and climbing has exhausted me. I am woken by heavy rain, loud thunder and lightning but delighted because I know it will clear the air. Several people have already pulled out of the race during Day 1 because of the intense sun, humidity, and altitude sickness.

The next morning, I wake at 4.15am and get ready. Based on Day 1, I am feeling slightly nervous about timing. I need to make the climb of 795m to checkpoint 6 in just two hours with a further ascent of 1,100m to reach 4,560m then back down, all by 1pm. The first part of the climb takes us through a forest then the terrain on the upper part of the mountain changes to soft scree. It is slippery in parts and the slope gets steeper. I reach the peak and look out at the mountains behind but don't hang around and make it down to checkpoint 7 by 10.50am. As I descend some runners are still toiling up through the soft, slippery shale. This is the hardest part of the race.

Onwards. The next two hills are long ascents. The climb seems to continue forever. We reach the top then head down to a large dry riverbed for a few kilometers. Running on the smooth round riverbed rocks is hard so eventually most of us give up and just walk. After passing checkpoint 8 the route passes through trees and beautiful wildflowers. I run alongside Milk Lake with crystal marine water and white sand. Suddenly large drops of rain start falling and rapidly become heavy.

I carry on running and am not far from an emergency checkpoint when I hear a shout to go and shelter. I huddle underneath a canopy with other runners and a few hikers. Thunder booms around us and the rain intensifies. I start to shiver and wrap myself in an emergency foil blanket.

Above the clouds at 4560m in Yunnan Province, China

Other runners do the same. There is a fear that the race will be suspended but after 90 minutes the rain stops and we are allowed to continue. The sun returns and quickly dries out the land. I skip over puddles and get my energy to run again. Even the warning sign about bears and boars doesn't bother me.

I reach checkpoint 9 to a cheery reception of ladies from the local village committee who seem unfazed by the recent downpour under their flimsy awning canopy. Just another 10k to checkpoint 10. The route is pretty flat following old tracks and with large puddles left by the rain I reach checkpoint 10. The lady on the stand encourages us to take lots of snacks because the next section is tough.

During the final part of the route, obedient cattle with their bells clanging stop to let me across the path as they head home. I cross a field, climb a steep bank, and then run across the grassy area that the race is sharing with locals offering pony rides.

Milk Lake near Jade Dragon Snow Mountain, Yunnan Province, China

Despite my concerns about altitude and timing, I have made it! After two days I come 8th out of the 35 women (11th on day one and 5th on day two). My achievement isn't my ranking but completing a race at high altitude — this is the dragon I need to tame.

Note regarding acclimatization:

With just five days between two 100k races and with the second starting 2,700m above the first what do you do to recover and rest?

After the karst cave race, for me the first question is whether to fly or take a train from Leye in Guangxi Province to Lijiang in neighbouring Yunnan Province. Since I am tired from my 22hr 101k, I opt for the train and also conscious that the gradual increase in elevation is better for acclimatizing compared with flying. Lijiang sits at 2,400m. For me, the effects of elevation are generally mild and but still noticeable with mild heart flutters and at night it is more difficult to sleep.

I finish my Leye race early on Monday morning. On Tuesday I walk approximately 10k around Lijiang. On Wednesday I do a short 8k hike climbing 600m (to 3,000m above sea level) up a nearby hill called Maanshan. The path is overgrown on the way up but on the way down I find a clearer path. The purpose of the hike is simply to climb and acclimatize, not to do distance. However, the real joy of the route is the discovery of so many beautiful wildflowers. On Thursday I go to Yuhu Village and do a short climb and 15k run. On Friday I rest. So overall during the week, I balance recovering from the previous race with acclimatizing to altitude.

6 WILD SAGE ON THE SOLSTICE

It has been raining all morning and it is a literal dampner on the mood as we walk to the start line of the Yunhai CTT 168k, which means 'Sea of Clouds', part of the 2024 Chicheng Ultra Trail. Early afternoon we set off through the northern Chinese town of Chicheng 200km north of Beijing, splashing through puddles. After a couple of kilometers, we head up a track with small neatly planted pine trees on one side and fruit plants on the other.

As the sky brightens, the mood lightens and the beauty of the land takes over. Sitting 1,000m above sea level after the long, dry winter when temperatures drop up to -30C° and the landscape turns brown, the greenery has returned with a sense of freshness. We continue to climb and the terrain turns to heath. Tiny wildflowers and berries grow among the rocks, and the damp air is infused by the strong scent of wild sage.

By mid-afternoon, the sun has returned. The latitude of Northern China benefits from longer daylight hours than the south of the country and for me the extra daylight is welcome — I know I will only have around eight hours of running in darkness.

Most of the checkpoints are set up in small countryside villages consisting of one-storey, honey-coloured brick houses with yards and small vegetable gardens. All the houses face south so that they benefit from the sun. Elderly villagers sit outdoors chatting in groups and calling out and cheering as we run through. The land connecting the villages ranges from disused, overgrown tracks with hard, uneven, cracked ruts dried in the strong sunshine to soft, steep, crumbly earth through woods and rocky riverbed-like areas where water finds its way down a valley in no fixed way — sometimes in flash floods.

Wild sage-covered hills near Chicheng, Hubei Province, China

Night falls and the most incredible full moon rises — it is the midsummer solstice. Thunder rumbles in the distance and light drops of rain start to fall — it feels refreshing after the 30+C° temperature of the afternoon. Lightning flashes dart around the silhouettes of the hills in the moonlight. It is magical and I continue running through the night, energized by the moon.

Just before dawn, I arrive at a checkpoint. I feel tired but revive myself with a bowl of watery rice porridge and pickles, plus some coffee. It sounds like an odd combination, but at that moment it is both hydrating and warming. I head out of the village yet I don't get far before tiredness hits. It is 5am and I have been going for 16hrs. I feel cold and wrap an emergency blanket around myself, lie down at the edge of a maize field, and set my alarm for ten minutes. I awake to the sound of my alarm. I feel groggy but force myself to move again.

Moon rising on the solstice, Chicheng, Hebei Province, China

The sun is white behind a layer of mist, but by 7am it has risen and is strong. Cows graze over wide meadows. These animals are incredibly agile, climbing up steep slopes, munching on small trees, and lounging at the top of hills. The route continues down past banks of short flowering bushes to wider pastures. I hear cries of shepherds gathering their goats and sheep together. Beautiful dark horses with their coats glistening in the sun canter around, excited by the strong wind blowing across the lower grasslands.

I leave a checkpoint and head straight up a hill to reach 1,700m. Routes in China always go directly uphill with no zigzagging. The strong wind on one side of the mountain makes it feel cold but woodland areas break the wind. As I continue to climb, on my left side I become aware of large moss-covered stones in a line all the way up the hillside. The piles of stones then become a neatly built wall in some sections. The line of wall stays with me, and then huge mounds of stones appear. I am focused on climbing in the bright sun and strong wind to reach the top of the mountain but curious about the stones. These stones form a section of the Great Wall with former lookout towers called Dushikou, which was built between the mountains and the grasslands around 1,500AD and was the site of countless battles. The wall looks different from the main Great Wall because it was built as a single wall, contrasting the much better-known dual-wall structure.

The vastness of these areas makes it hard to have a sense of distance I sometimes wonder if I am actually making any progress. Reaching 7m in parts, the drop off one side of the wall is dramatic and sweeps down a hillside. Finally, I reach the summit with a remains of a large watchtower before my descent begins. I return to the grasslands and early afternoon reach the second checkpoint for changing supplies. I have another ten-minute nap — this time in a room with mats. A couple of other runners do the same.

I set off again. The afternoon sun feels very strong and bright and I am moving slowly in the sunshine. I don't see any other runners on the route. After a while, I hear a voice of encouragement behind me - "*Jiayou, jiaoyou*" - literally meaning "add oil". A young 100k runner comes alongside me smiling and saying "Come on little big sister" (an affectionate reference to both my height and age). She reflects the tone of everybody in this race — always encouraging and enthusiastic. I watch as she disappears up the hill with incredible grace and ease. I try to mimic her style but am simply much slower!

I float past some more checkpoints and darkness starts to fall again. One of the sections between two villages is paved with white concrete. Although it is flat, I find it hard to run on this surface after the undulating trails, but I have just two checkpoints left before the end of the race, so I keep going. An elderly farmer in the fields says sympathetically and genuinely, "You must be tired". I look at the fields of vegetables he is tilling and feel embarrassed recognizing the physicality of his daily work.

There is one 750m hill left to conquer. At the insistence of one of the volunteers, I eat some noodles, head out of the checkpoint, and start climbing again. The path becomes vague across moorland punctuated with short pine trees, thorn bushes, and large manmade holes in the earth waiting for a tree to be planted. I can see a few lights moving up the hill in the distance. The lights dart around and keep disappearing. I discover it is because the greenery is dense and the path has become rocky. Then I see the arc of lamps hitting the clouds. A luminous tent is like a beacon lit up on the hillside for rescue services.

Sunset, Chicheng, Hebei Province, China

By this point we have left the vegetation, the strong wind has returned and it is raining lightly. The reflective markers of the course have disappeared, and I feel disoriented. I am looking out across a sea of clouds. I check my GPS and follow a route that doesn't feel instinctively correct but eventually, I catch a marker dancing in the wind in the beam of my headtorch.

I reach the final checkpoint and with just 6k to go, everybody is united by a sense of wanting to finish. We run, climb, and head down the final hill on an ungraded road of soft sand. After 35 hours 47 minutes, 168k and 6,950m, I finish 8th out of the women.

This brings my accumulated race total for the first six months of the year to an auspicious 888km – eight is a lucky number in China. What have I learned during this time? I must keep training, getting stronger, and improve on my weaknesses such as my climbing speed. In the words of a different sage, the Chinese general and strategist Sun-Tzu "We are not fit to lead an army on the march unless we are familiar with the face of the country - its mountains and forests, its pitfalls and precipices, its marshes and swamps."

7 WILDFLOWERS & FIRS

The Chinese philosopher Laozi famously said, "A journey of 1,000 miles begins with a single step." I discovered this to be true when I realized I had run 1,054k of races and climbed a total elevation of 5.7 times the height of Mount Everest since the start of 2024.

My ninth race of the year was a 168k trail located near Zhangjiakou around 200k north of Beijing in the scenic area of Chongli, the main location for the Beijing 2022 Winter Olympics. Situated in the mountains and best known for skiing, the highest point is around 2100m. In winter, temperatures can drop to around −30C and in summer it is around +30C. With a very dry climate, the arid brown hills from the winter are transformed into lush, green meadows covered with wildflowers in summer. For this reason, I am excited to go back to Chongli.

Chongli is also where I completed my first 50k and 100k races, so the area has a special place in my heart. Returning this time for the 168k, I notice that the town has expanded due to the Winter Games and there is a high-speed train station nearby, plus a new highway direct to Beijing.

Early in the afternoon before the race, rain starts to fall and as puddles form near the race start line, I contemplate running in waterproofs. Thankfully, just a few minutes before the early evening start, the rain stops and over 600 runners head off. After running through town, the road turns to a mud track and we start heading up into the hills past cattle. The path becomes narrow and this section forces the runners into a single file. Darkness falls around 8.30pm so we have around 8–9 hours of darkness ahead of us, but this isn't the challenge.

Wild flowers early morning near Chongli, Hebei Province, China

During the past few weeks, there has been torrential rain and we frequently encounter deep, slippery mud on tracks and steep hills. Everybody is sliding as they make their way down the slopes. It is impossible to go fast and nobody escapes without getting spattered in mud causing generally hilarity. My shoes are caked with mud and heavy as I run.

The hills of the route are all around 2,000-2,100m. At night, the temperature cools to around 15 degrees and I wear a hat and gloves because the air is damp and it is windy. It isn't cold but I shiver each time

I stop at a station to refill my water and grab some warm food such as rice congee.

Hills near Chongli, Hebei Province, China

The next morning, the temperature rises with the sun. The combination of mild altitude, humidity, and strong sunshine takes a toll and causes over one-third of the runners to ultimately pull out of the race.

It is late afternoon and I feel as if I have been moving slowly all day. I reach checkpoint 11 (out of 16) and see another runner, Eric, whom I met during a previous 168k race. We don't know each other well but finished our last race together. He is just about to leave the checkpoint. He looks at me and says let's run together and keep moving. I know I need somebody to help and encourage me as we move towards the second evening.

I lead and we head downhill. Tiredness is really setting in and I know I will have to rest. I opt for short 5 or 10-minute naps to revive me enough to keep going, although in retrospect I should perhaps have had longer rests. Through silver birch forests, down ski slopes, up over hills of wildflowers and fir trees, we work as a pair to motivate each other.

Outline of fir trees against the sunrise. Hebei Province, China

Whilst I am faster running downhill, Eric is steady uphill and keeps me moving whenever I am thinking about slowing down. He is particularly good at cajoling me on flat ground which I find less interesting. Our approach seems to work — we maintain a steady pace and overtake many runners who are flagging and visibly tired but nervous about stopping to sleep in case they can't wake up.

As the sun rises for the second time, we find a paved road at the top of a hill and meet runners from the 70k race as the routes merge. Compared with our muddy clothes, they look incredibly fresh, and clean and exude energy. We run together on the paved road then let them pass when the route reverts to narrow paths and try to absorb some of their energy to reach our finish. The sun is becoming fierce, and we hug any shade that we see. Eventually, we navigate our final hill overlooking Chongli. We descent leaving the wildflowers behind, and head back into town along a flat road. With encouragement from locals on the street, we arrive after 41 hours 40 mins, 168.1k, and 8,788m total elevation.

From the 600-plus runners, 423 finished including 85 women. I finish 8th in my age category and 200th overall. Am I satisfied? Well, eight is a lucky number in China!

8 MUD OR FINE PORCELAIN?

Ninghai was first recorded as a county in 240AD with its history of civilization stretching back to the stone age. Located in China's Eastern Zhejiang Province, Ninghai (宁海) means "pacified from the sea," referring to its location upriver protecting it from the East China Sea. Instead, the terrain is a sea of greenery. With a rich history in Chinese opera, fine porcelain and, bizarrely, the production center for 80% of the world's binder clips (fun fact), we are certainly not the first people to explore these trails. In fact, there is a distinct aura that we are treading on ancient land.

It is over five years since I have been to Ultra-Trail Ninghai and I remember the crisp morning of the previous race with frost on the ground and clear blue skies, so I am keen to return and run again. The 105k group sets off from the grand West Gate of Ninghai at 6am and moves up into the hills. Despite an incredibly hot summer this year, there is no direct sun and although the paths are slightly slippery following recent rain, the temperature feels perfect. The route takes us through pine trees mentioned by Confucian writers, bamboo forests, tea plantations, ancient stone paths used for centuries to connect villages, and steep paths heading directly up the mountainside. The race is going smoothly.

In the afternoon, just as I leave a checkpoint, there is a bag check to ensure we have the mandatory gear including a waterproof jacket and headtorches. I view the checks simply as a precaution, but near the top of the next hill drops of rain start to fall so I will be using my waterproof soon enough. The rain soon becomes heavier with no sign of stopping. The next checkpoint is a station for changing clothes and supplies. My trail shoes and clothes are damp and sweaty in spite of wearing a jacket so I need to change. Setting out again in dry shoes, fresh clothes, and long leggings, but the rain becomes even heavier.

West Gate, Ninghai, Zhejiang Province, China

Although it isn't late, the rain is making the sky dark as I head up a paved road with small waves of water flowing downhill towards me.

The road returns to earthen trail. The sustained rain is rapidly changing the entire race, not because it is wet, but because of the smooth layer of clay that coats everything. Thick mud clings to my shoes making my movement heavy. Normally earth falls off my soles as I run but the clay sticks and clogs the tread of my shoes making it difficult to move lightly. A fine layer cakes the broken, ancient stone paths. Heading downhill becomes almost comedic as my grip fails, and I slide treacherously and struggle to keep my balance. Ahead, my view is white mist but when I look down, I see yet more shiny mud as my feet slip down the hillside. I am not alone, and everybody is grappling with the conditions. In the darkness, runners support each other, pointing out the best routes to navigate, and safely climb or descend the hills.

Hills above Ninghai, Zhejiang Province, China

I have 30k of the race left and suddenly have a flash of clarity about the true meaning of endurance. The deluge has lasted for seven hours making the course slow and difficult. At around 1am, I feel almost overwhelmed by desire to sleep. I pause at a checkpoint and see some people quitting, but I want to keep going. I find that despite the tiredness, being out on the hillside and looking at the dark outline of the hills against the sky is just magical and entrancing. Hearing the bird cries, and sounds of creaking bamboo combined with the scent of the pines is simply a privilege even if I am moving slowly. I persist. At 22 hours and 19 minutes, I cross the finish line.

Out of 1,097 runners, 835 finish. I am 515th overall, 85th woman, 7th in my age group. I look at my medal and my muddy, clay-covered feet. For centuries, people have been wandering these hills and turning the clay into earthenware and porcelain. This has been a tough race, and in many ways a bit of a blur battling the harsh conditions, fine porcelain only comes from refining clay. With every race, we refine our ability to endure and become better runners!

Ultra-Trail Ninghai by UTMB is now part of the UTMB World Series and just celebrated its 10th anniversary.

9 BEAR GROWLS ABOVE THE CLOUDS

It has taken me four years to get to Tengchong, Yunnan Province, China for the Anta Guanjun Gaoligong Ultra 168, so I am excited to see the return of this race following a hiatus due to Covid. Situated just 50k from the border with Myanmar, Tengchong is almost directly north of, and slightly further west than Chiangmai in northern Thailand. The Gaoligong Mountains are a sub-range of the southern Hengduan Mountain Range which connects the Tibetan Plateau with the Yunnan-Guizhou Plateau, and the area has rich greenery and fertile farmland.

Sitting at 1,640m, the town of Tengchong, where the race begins, has been a trading centre for centuries and is the last stop in China on the less famous Southern Silk Road to Burma and on to India when traders would trade tea, silk, tobacco, and bamboo in long caravans of horses. So, wearing our trail vests and carrying our supplies, our journey is certainly easier than those before us.

Setting out from the main square in the early morning light, we leave Tengchong below and climb up through woods and onto heath. I find a shaggy Bactrian camel offering rides but head on past with a smile to reach the first checkpoint before following abandoned tracks and descending into dense jungle. Mist swirls and the ground is slightly muddy, but as we hop across small streams and rocks the sun appears and we enjoy the rich canopy and bird cries around us. As we climb higher, the earth changes colour from brown to deep red and the elevation gives us views across the forest-covered hills. Lower in the valleys, rice harvest is in full swing and many people are out on the paddy terraces. As we arrive at the checkpoint, ladies from local minority tribes greet us with folksongs and drumming.

Clouds rising in Gaoligong, Yunnan Province, China

We climb to 2,394m before descending to 1,300m to start the main climb of the race to 2,614m with some up and down along the way. Night descends and we rise into the clouds. Moisture from the cloud drips onto the bushes and trees as we slowly ascend over the broken rocks of the ancient paths, then descend on earthen paths strewn with pine needles through pine trees and bamboo. Recent rain has made the ground squelchy and visibility in the clouds is just a couple of meters. Progress is slow. Suddenly I hear a growl and rustling in the bushes. I am expecting wild boar, but this sounds different. I am alone on the path. I pause to listen then continue on as fast as I can, without knowing exactly why. Not much further on, I discover why my instinct is telling me to speed up - I see a sign saying "Watch out for Sun Bears"! These bears grow to around

65kg and 1.2m in length. They apparently aren't really aggressive unless provoked but I don't plan to find out.

Having set out at 7.30am, after over 17 hours, at around 1am, the desire to sleep is overwhelming. I pass the highest point of the race and I allow myself to lie down and rest at the next checkpoint.

Corn harvest in Yunnan Province, China

Whilst I am moving the weather doesn't feel cold, but now I am drained. I put on my waterproof jacket and woolly hat. With my hood up against the wind, heat slowly returns to my body. I am still feeling weary and I can't run so I just walk for a couple of kilometres to maintain momentum. A temporary refreshment station had been added at this point which is welcome because apparently I am not alone in my dipping energy levels and many other runners have been feeling hungry. With a warm bowl of noodles inside me I am revived but I am also conscious that this tiredness is costing me time.

Rather than seeing my arrival time at checkpoints improve, it is getting closer to the cutoff times, so I really need to move. After a few hours, daylight returns, and the light boosts my energy level. Suddenly I am able to flow again run freely through the forests. The landscape changes and the sun shines as I look down from above the clouds. We climb again, this time through tobacco plantations and the sunlight dances through the trees. The beauty of the path is intoxicating and energizing. The terrain and flora remind me of my second early morning in Betong and realize that Tengchong is geographically almost directly north but even further west.

Early morning above the clouds, Gaoligong, Yunnan Province, China

I start to make up time. There are just 27k left. As darkness falls for the second time, I have a bowl of rice porridge and start to ascend again along narrow, windy mountain paths. We head through a village and along a paved road. Now just 6k from the finish line I climb up into the mist one final time. I can't see the path but follow my instinct. In the blur I see a fire and find two mountain rescue men who point the way. Perhaps due to its proximity to the ancient town of Heshun, the route becomes a wide caravan track and I descend over the overgrown flagstones. A final 100m to ascend and then down to the deserted, eerily quiet streets of Heshun. I follow the strobe lights of the finish line in the distance. At exactly 43 hours I cross the finish line - 171.7k with 8,848m total elevation. I am 50th overall and 14th among the women. During the next five hours, another 25 people cross the finish line. 50 don't finish.

Heshun (和顺) means 'peace and harmony'. This perfectly sums up my emotions after finishing such an incredibly beautiful and at times almost mystical trail.

10 THE FOUR SISTERS

It is 2am when I arrive for a bag check at the start line for the 2024 Kailas Ultra Tour Siguniang 75k race. Siguniang (The Four Sisters), sits at 3,160m in the mountains of Sichuan Province in Western China. The range is part of the Qionglai Mountain range which runs North-South in the Ngawa Tibetan and Qiang Autonomous Prefecture.

As the race begins there is a cold wind and the thin air of altitude is making it feel colder. We set off and climb up a muddy track towards the first mountain peak at a lofty 4,503m. As we rise higher the route narrows and the land sparkles with frost beneath the moonlight. After crossing a fast-flowing river balancing on tree trunks, the climb properly begins. We leap across a stream and one of my feet plunges into the icy water. The temperature has dropped well below zero and I am wearing a balaclava and hat, thermals, a merino wool layer, and two pairs of gloves but this still isn't sufficient below my thick waterproof jacket. The nozzles of my soft water bottles are icing over so I sip water just to prevent them freezing completely. Sometimes in winter I put electrolytes or something sugary into my water just to prevent the bottles from freezing but I prefer to drink water and take electrolyte tablets separately.

My hands are feeling cold. I climb up the icy path keen to reach the checkpoint at the top of the mountain as soon as possible. This is critical because the cutoff time is very tight. By the time I arrive at the summit at around 7am I am shivering. My lips are turning blue, my speech has been reduced to gibberish, and my hands are tingling with pain. The temperature at the top of the mountain has dropped to minus ten plus windchill. An amazing volunteer gives me hot water then realizes I am still cold. She ushers me into a tent beside a stove, brings me soup and nurses me back to life. At that moment, I truly believe that the feeling in my hands has gone forever, and I don't want to move from this spot. I have a moment of delirium. Sitting opposite me a Tibetan horseman wearing a fine black woollen dell (a traditional long tunic with a silk sash at the waist) and the serene expression of someone completely at peace with the mountains looks sympathetic. He assures me that this is one of the highest and coldest points of the race and wishes me luck. Amazingly just as quickly as I deteriorated, I recover.

View of Mt Siguniang, Sichuan Province, China

As I head down the mountain in daylight, like everybody else I wear crampons over my trail shoes so that I don't slip on the ice and snow. Runners are still coming up the hill towards me. They wear an expression of intensity knowing there are only a few minutes left before the cutoff time – I am relieved to be moving on to the next stage. There is no vehicle access so if they don't make it, they will have to plod down the way they came back to Siguniang village. The only other option is to hire one of the hardy small ponies but the path down the mountain is steep so it probably isn't a comfortable option.

Valley beside Mt Siguniang, Sichuan Province, China.

The sun is rising with a clear blue sky and occasional pink clouds. I head towards the next checkpoint past crystal clear lakes and frozen bushes. A gradual climb begins. I have lost some time at the previous checkpoint by staying to warm up and so I need to press on but my movement feels slightly laboured due to the altitude. I am not the only person with struggling as we head up a path to reach the next checkpoint at 4,328m beside a turquoise crystal lake passing yaks grazing on the winter grass.

This race is in a very remote area so all the checkpoints are set up by transporting tents, gas and supplies by horse caravan. Some supplies are also delivered using drones – traditional and modernity together.

Rhino Sea, Siguniang, Sichuan Province, China.

The route is signposted using flag on thin stakes dotted across the landscape. Sometimes following an existing path, in other places, the flags simply show the specific course for the race. We descend then climb up small rocks on a steep and slow-going path to reach the next checkpoint called Double Sea (双海子) at 4,613m.

This is the highest and most challenging mountain of the race. With loose rocks underfoot and the steep gradient everybody has to simply keep moving. The view is spectacular with snow-covered mountains all around but there is no time to linger and enjoy the panorama. Due to the remote location of this race, the cut-off times are tight so everybody is feeling pressure to reach the summit and move to the next point as quick as possible. I pass some people on the way up and as I return down the mountain, I see them still struggling to climb. These runners aren't unfit

– ten hours into the race they are simply challenged by the thin air, altitude and tiredness.

After some hot porridge at the next checkpoint, another steep climb begins providing incredible views across the valley. The final mountain at higher altitude is exhausting for everybody. At times it is only possible to take a few steps before taking a rest.

Double Sea, Siguniang, Sichuan Province, China.

On the horizon, we see the silhouette of somebody disappearing over the brow of the hill. There is a checkpoint hiding out of sight which marks the point where we descend to 3,300m. From the checkpoint there is a spectacular luminescent view of Siguniang in the early evening sun. When we drop to lower altitude, the track becomes very muddy as we follow a river, gradually ascending again. The track continues and broadens. The temperature has dropped because it is nighttime. I pass a sign warning to be vigilant about bears but weighed by tiredness I ignore it and just focus on the path ahead.

Finally, I reach the penultimate checkpoint beside a monastery. Time is not on my side. In the dark with just my headtorch to show me the way I climb uphill alongside the white plaster wall of the temple with its red, shuttered frames beneath the noise of prayer flags flapping in the strong wind. I climb 300m through bushes and finally spy the finish line far down in the valley below. I descend as fast as I can from 3,600m to 3,160m – worried I won't make it. With its extreme cold, strong wind and high altitude, this race has really pushed me physically but I finally cross the finish line after 23 hours and 40 minutes with just 20 minutes to spare.

Receiving a *katak* at the end of the race, a traditional Tibetan ceremonial scarf offered as a sign of respect. Credit: Ultra Tour

At 111th, I am one of the last people to finish out of the original 223 runners. Only 51% of the competitors complete the race. While certainly not my finest race performance I am happy simply to complete this challenging trail and learn more about running at altitude and extreme conditions. I originally signed up for the 75k race thinking this would slightly less demanding than the longer 100k route but afterwards discover that this course is recognized as being much tougher in terms of gradient and terrain.

Early the next morning as I depart from the village, I catch a glimpse of snow-covered Mt Siguniang majestically rising out of thin air against the pink clouds, waiting for me next year!

11 ISLAND LIFE ON STILTS

Leaving the bustle of Hong Kong Island during rush hour and arriving at Mui Wo village on south side of Lantau Island by evening ferry as the sun sets is probably one of the most magical ways to arrive at a race. It is almost dark as I walk to the race area and the quietness of island life with the sound of the sea lapping on the beach sets the tone for the 2024 TransLantau by UTMB® 120 (100M).

At 10pm we set off into the darkness and gradually climb higher on a mix of rocks and level sand paths. The first major hill and highest of the race is called Sunset Peak at 886m providing 360-degree views across to the twinkling lights of Mainland China and Hong Kong Island. The weather feels perfect. Although it is early November it isn't cold even at the peak. Throughout the night we jump over rocks and follow sandy paths connecting villages along the shoreline. The route traces the entire outline of Lantau Island from the isolated Western-most point of Hong Kong to the busy international airport and the ferry terminal to the Greater Bay Area.

By late morning we arrive at the pretty traditional village of Tai O with little fishermen's houses on stilts above the water. We follow the ancient trail connecting the village to Tung O. After hugging the coastline, we climb steeply up over 2,000 stone steps and wooden platforms to reach the centre of the island. The hill is just 546m but feels higher. We head down towards island's famous Po Lin Monastery with its 34m bronze Buddha statue gleaming in the early evening light.

Much of the path is overgrown. We continue uphill for the final major climb of 685m. It is getting dark and the broken steps and rocks on the path are getting bigger requiring us to clamber between boulders rather than run. By the time we reach the summit mist has descended, heavy rain sweeps in on strong winds and visibility is reduced to just a couple of meters. I struggle to see any markers and feel disorientated. I rely on my GPS map for the first time during the race. It shows a route but doesn't feel intuitive and I feel slightly off course in the long-wet grass and swirling mist. Despite feeling slightly lost I keep following some kind of path and which eventually leads me downhill. The rain intensifies, the rocks become more slippery and the steep sandy paths turn to mud.

A path on Lantau Island, Hong Kong

It is past midnight on the second night of the race and tiredness is taking over. I pause for a moment standing up as the rain pours down. I jolt and wake up with no idea how long I have been asleep whilst still standing on my feet. Small red flashing lights highlight a turning off a road into the undergrowth. There is around 8k to the finish line. The rain isn't giving up and neither am I. I slosh through puddles on the narrow path struggling to see the signage and hoping I am on the right course. In some parts the rocks are so large I am lowering my body down dangling my feet and hoping to reach the ground with a small jump as I land in muddy puddles. Elsewhere, I have to pull myself up and crawl onto the wet stones.

Eventually the path turns to paving. A road heads steeply uphill. Reflecting my own energy levels, my headtorch is wavering. In the darkness I switch to use my second spare headtorch under the trees dripping with rainwater. Finally, the bay where I started over 30 hours before comes into view. I can see the ferry terminal. Steps lead me back down to sea level and a paved path beside the beach.

After over seven of constant rain and a total of 31 hours 32 minutes on the course I return to a drenched finish line. 108th overall and 18th woman. Only 54% of the original 346 runners finish. Battling the brutal rain and strong winds has been tough.

Reaching a wet finish line during the TransLantau HongKong. Credit: Sportograf

I join exhausted and bedraggled runners slumped in the ferry terminal wrapped in their emergency blankets awaiting the first boat at dawn back to Hong Kong Island. I board, close my eyes, and fall instantly asleep awaking as the ferry berths to see skyscrapers towering above.

12 ELEPHANTS & GOLD

It is early evening when I land in Chiang Mai in Northern Thailand, almost 700k directly south of Tengchong in Yunnan Province, China but much more humid it feels much warmer than the official 27 degrees Celsius. The plane gently descends over rice paddies and red roof houses onto the Mae Ping River basin surrounded by the Thai Highlands.

I am participating in the UTMB® World Series – Asia Pacific Major Thailand. I have registered for the Trans-Int 160 which is in fact 172k with a total elevation of 8,980m. The name of the race refers to Doi Inthanon, the tallest mountain in Thailand. The other race distances have locally inspired names such as the Elephant 100 and Hmong 50. The Hmong people are the second largest hill tribe in Thailand.

Four UTMB World Series Majors are held each year and are considered the pinnacle events across the Americas, Europe, Asia-Pacific and the Oceania regions. So many of the world's top trail runners from Asia-Pacific as well as Europe and the US are participating. I may not be a top runner but feel flattered to be invited to a pre-event activity for elite runners.

This is an 'A to B' race and starts at a Buddhist monastery called Wat Nam Tong which is a 70k drive from Chiang Mai so I need to get to the race bus transporting runners to the start point. At 6.30am the roads are quiet and there are no taxis available, so I order a moped driver to pick me up. He arrives with a spare helmet and we head off along a deserted highway clutching my three race bags (one running vest and two drop bags) plus running sticks.

Wat Nam Tong, Chiang Mai, Thailand

Wat Nam Tong looks opulent with white plaster and gold glistening in the sun. Unusually for a race, the start is at 10am and the sun feels strong. It is officially only 28 degrees but 'feels like' 34 degrees with the typical intensity of Thailand's sun. All the runners relax in the shadows of the monastery buildings dozing and catching some final moments of rest before the race.

The route begins with a 1,534m climb. After the first couple of kilometers past traditional wooden houses the road becomes a narrow path and trees offer some welcome canopy. Light dances through the branches and the forest floor is mainly dry and covered with large autumnal leaves and wild flowers. The route undulates as we steadily rise into the mountains.

Wat Huay Pla Kung, Chiang Mai Credit: Running Connect

Although we set off in a flurry from the start-line the heat soon slows everybody, and the runners quickly settle into a steady rhythm. This race has attracted people from all over Asia as well as some Europeans and Americans. By around 20k a few runners are trying to push ahead but we are still early in the race and the slopes are becoming steeper. Some people overtake me and vice-versa but I know that for me, trying to maintain my own steady pace is most important.

As we climb up the mountain the landscape changes to denser jungle with rich ochre-coloured earth and a mix of fir trees and rhododendrons. The sounds of the jungle remind me of Betong earlier in the year with bird calls and the loud frenetic buzz of insects. The aromas of the jungle are a mix of pine, damp earth and a slightly sweet fragrance. As we climb, I realise that the cap of my soft water bottle on my running vest has broken and water is leaking over everything. Thankfully I have packed a spare bottle.

We climb through the day following winding rocky paths and jump across streams. When night falls I find the darkness strangely energizing. High up on the hillside we pass the lights of polytunnels growing vegetables, strawberries and flowers. Without the sun sapping my energy I find it easier to run perturbed only by small bats flying towards me attracted by the beam of my headtorch. I maintain my flow by chasing along behind a few runners and this helps to keep me moving.

After a night of clambering over rocks and skipping across streams in the dark, I pause to rest on a bench in a village at around 6am. Just a few minutes later I jolt awake. The world is quiet. Nobody is around. Feeling slightly disoriented I follow the marker ribbons unsure of which direction I am going. Dawn is just breaking and the dark fields start to glow revealing neat rows of vegetables. I run along a road and am startled to see an enormous elephant silhouetted against the early morning light. I then realise this is an elephant sanctuary, and the home of this majestic, dignified animal.

Not much further along I find a checkpoint which is also a change station and realise I could have slept on a camp bed rather than sitting upright on a bench! After restocking my nutrition, I press on with a new climb. By the second day, the runners have become spread out along the trail and I am seeing some of the same people, each following their speed and rhythm.

I start climbing. At 2,061m, the next mountain is the highest of the race. The sun is still low in the sky but the climbing feels hard. I meet a runner disconsolately returning downhill. He is one of the top runners but has decided to pull out of the race because it is 'too hard'. I become worried about what might lie ahead but the landscape is so pretty with red rocks, pine trees, and silver flecks gleaming on the earth. I keep moving.

Dawn breaks near Chiang Mai

I feel slow and assume that the other runners must be in front and further ahead than I thought, but I know there is still enough time for me to complete the race. I reach the top with a sense of relief and head down to Wat Huay Pla Kung. The temple area feels serene. I refill my water and continue.

My legs feel heavy and the second afternoon of climbing is tough. I join up with some other runners and the motivation to keep moving is mutual as the terrain becomes steeper still. I lean on my poles to pull myself up the slopes. We are all choosing our own routes across the rocks and dry earth that provide shade rather than the most direct route. Heading downhill provides respite. I see a sign for the next checkpoint and runners from the 100k race start to appear as our routes merge. It has just got dark and we head up a steep hill to be rewarded by a magical view of Wat Ban Pong (The White Pagoda). I am blown away by finding this magnificent temple rising out of the darkness. It is so large that it can be seen from Chiang Mai 17k away.

Near Khun Klang Village, Chiang Mai. Credit: Running Connect

Now for the final big climb of the race, 1,000m up to Wat Phra That Doi Suthep. Tiredness is affecting me and my mind is playing tricks creating a weird sense of excitement about reaching the temple. I see lots of imaginary people and buildings as I climb up this path before realizing they are just shadows created by leaves. In the darkness I feel I am making no progress on this mountain. It seems to go on forever but there is no option to escape. It is around 5.5k to the summit then a further 2.5k winding along a path to the next checkpoint at the Doi Pui Research Station. This research station is focused on plant life, in particular the impact of deforestation caused by the Hmong people clearing some of the highest land to grow vegetables. We pass Wat Phra That Doi Suthep with its gold tiles glittering in the darkness then return to a forest path.

After a couple of kilometres, the path reaches a paved road winding downhill. With just 13k left, I run down the hill, pass the penultimate checkpoint and keep going. There are occasional glimpses of Chiang Mai lit up down below in the valley. Finally, we are at the bottom of the mountain. I can see the finish line illuminated with strobe lights in the darkness. I follow the final few markers and arrive at the finish line. Out of 359 starters, there are 233 finishers and 126 DNFs. I am happy to discover I am 91st overall, 16th woman and, without being aware of it, have moved up from fourth to first place in my age category.

As a result of this race, a few days later I receive a message from UTMB® offering me a place at the world finals, Ultra-Trail Mont-Blanc 2025 in Chamonix, France. Can I dare to call myself a trail runner?

Arriving at the finish line of the Trans-Int 160, Chiang Mai, Thailand. Credit: Running Connect

13 KIT ESSENTIALS

I am often asked about my 'kit' or rather equipment and supplies. Like any sport, there are pricey and cheap options but for an average runner, safety needs to always be a priority – dehydration, hunger, injury, tiredness, change in weather or even wild animals are real potential dangers and need to be taken seriously! An expensive t-shirt is unlikely to make you run any faster but a decent waterproof jacket and merino wool layer might save your life. Obviously the more remote the trail, the more precautions you need to take. So here is my kit list:

KIT BASICS:

- Trail vest
- Trail shoes
- T-shirt
- Shorts
- Merino wool socks
- Compression sleeves
- Running poles (folding or collapsible)
- Two 500ml soft water bottles plus a spare
- 1 foldable cup
- 1 collapsible bowl
- Collapsible cutlery
- 1 trash bag
- Emergency blanket (double sided)
- Whistle
- First-aid kit with band aids, crepe bandage, ibuprofen, alcohol swabs, tweezers etc
- Two headtorches + wires for charging (sometimes three)
- Watch + charging cable
- Battery pack
- Mobile phone + charging cable

- Sunscreen
- Sunglasses
- Chapstick / vaseline
- Nutrition (see next section)

HOT WEATHER

- Lightweight waterproof taped jacket (10,000 Schmerber)
- Cap
- Headband (standard size cut into two pieces)
- T-shirt
- Shorts
- Light leggings for night-time
- Arm sleeves (optional)
- Short gaiters (optional)
- Mosquito repellent

COLD WEATHER

- Heavyweight waterproof taped jacket (10,000 Schmerber) (below zero degrees Celsius)
- Thermals
- Windproof / waterproof leggings (sometimes two pairs)
- Gloves (two pairs)
- Woolen hat / balaclava
- Crampons (for ice or snow)

HOW TO PACK

Don't just throw all items into your bag. Separate items into individual waterproof 'dry' bags, or ziplock bags (all electronics in one bag, spare t-shirt in another bag etc). You might be wondering why? During a race your back will become wet with rain, dew and sweat so this is the best way to keep things dry. It also makes it faster to identify a specific item when you need it repack afterwards.

14 NUTRITION

What do I eat during races? Learning what to eat and how often is very personal remains a work in progress for me. However over long distances, nutrition and maintaining energy levels is essentially about managing and reducing tiredness and exhaustion. When I become too tired, my body stops processing water and food. If this happens, it is not conducive to completing a race.

Hydration is fundamental. I continually sip water drinking 100ml per kilometre. For example, during my race in Chiang Mai I drank around 16 litres of water plus nearly 4 litres of electrolytes and soft drinks during the 40 hours – but all of this was consumed in small sips. Some people like electrolyte drinks and will consume far more of these. For me, I find that salt and electrolyte tablets agree with me better than powders and pre-mixed drinks. Drinking too fast or too much water can lead to overhydration and then food isn't absorbed. At checkpoints I have generally have a small cup of an electrolyte drink or coke but I always listen to my body.

Food is a topic of personal preference, but the basic message is that it is essential to keep eating. Some people are able to get everything they need from sports gels. I personally don't use artificial gels but have found that fruit puree (various brands) and all-natural gels work well. In China checkpoints often provide rice or yellow millet porridge (congee) which is hydrating and filling as well as warming. As a backup I take sachets of dry porridge oats and instant coffee because there is usually hot water at checkpoints. Other options such as steamed bread or sliced bread and peanut butter are offered but I find these hard to eat when I am thirsty.

15 TRAINING

Without wishing to state the obvious, running regular ultra-marathons requires ongoing training. Professional athletes can dedicate their time to exercising and resting. For most however, the amount of time anybody can dedicate to training is a balance of ambition and goals plus personal choice minus commitments and responsibilities such as day jobs, looking after families and other interests.

For me, daily runs of 12-15k are fundamental. Once or twice a week I will do a longer run of 25k. So on average I will run 90-100k per week excluding races. This is around half the distance that professional athletes run.

In addition, I do HIIT (High Intensity Interval Training) which I believe helps my residual fitness and overall strength – this is particularly important as we get older. I also love mini-band exercises for helping with strength. I sometimes do yoga and enjoy it but always wish I had started it younger because although I know it is good for me, it tends to feel slightly like medicine.

I also think that there are many small things that contribute to our residual fitness – whether fast walking rather than using a car or using stairs rather than lifts. Use any opportunity to move!

16 REFLECTIONS FROM THE CAVE

On my trails this year I passed many lakes and crossed many streams. For me the stillness of a lake in early morning light and its complete mirror reflection as it reveals itself at dawn is one of the most magical moments of the day. Nevertheless, there is a certain irony in witnessing the renewal of nature as it creates a new day after battling tiredness through a long night and being at my most drained. They call it this the 'pain cave' – that point in a race when you have pushed yourself almost to the limits and the tiredness feels all-consuming. Yet in these tranquil moments when dawn breaks, the energy seems to return and the body is miraculously revitalized.

Of my 16 races I completed all except for one. What are the qualities and traits that make me keep going and go through the pain cave of extreme tiredness to arrive at a finish line? At a talk for TEDbyShibocun this year I attempted to explain this by referring to Angela Duckworth's definition of grit. She defines it as the combination of perseverance and passion over the long-term. This recognizes the benefits of consistently working at a skill to deliver results that far outweigh short-term triumphs. In trail running, grit is enabled and facilitated by consistent training and a long-term commitment to building up fitness blended with a passion for being outdoors in remote and beautiful places.

The compilation of this short book doesn't cover every spectacular moment on a trail but hopefully it captures the spirit of trail running which is essentially about the range of physical and mental challenges posed by terrain, weather and temperature. Underpinning this is a desire to be challenged, push through and improve for the next race.

Completing a race is important although not always possible. If it isn't possible for a reason such as exhaustion, injury or extreme weather then it is important to finish the next race. This creates a mentality of winning by finishing what you set out to do and is a lesson for life, not just trail running.

This year I have experienced extreme temperatures and varying weather conditions from torrential rain to searing sun. Training in all seasons is important – this tests yourself as well as your gear. It is better to discover that your waterproof jacket is leaking on a short run close to home rather than during a thunderstorm in the wild. You might be hot when you are running, and nobody wants to carry too much additional, seemingly unnecessary clothing but consider how cold you might get if you fall and need to wait for emergency services. Similarly, strong sun at altitude can quickly burn skin so covering up is also important.

The mountains are in control, not you. At a ceremony before our race in Gaoligong a local shaman offered blessings to the mountains for our safe return. We have to respect the mountains and do what they are telling us to do such as accepting changes in the weather or respecting the animals and environment.

Regardless of our age, trail running brings out the inner child in all of us as we clamber over rocks and through mud. The sheer joy of running in the hills is simply a privilege.

There is a general rule during races that everybody looks after each other. The friendship and support I have encountered during trail races is incredible. The short conversations or mutual words of encouragement when somebody is exhausted or just offering to accompany somebody on the trail through the night reflects an incredible spirit and community. Whilst I speak Chinese, I don't speak Japanese, Korean, Thai or Malay which I frequently hear on the trails. But the spirit transcends language. This helps us to climb out of the cave at the toughest moments.

Looking back at the year, women have typically accounted for 20% of the runners for 100k and 168k/100mile races. I hope that this will increase in the future.

I end 2024 ranked among the top 10 British female one hundred-milers with a place at Ultra-Trail Mont-Blanc 168k. More trailing around Asia lies ahead no doubt with more mud, sweat and a few bears!

ABOUT THE AUTHOR

Harriet Gaywood moved to China from the UK in the 1990s and built a career in public relations and communications. Holding four separate masters degrees in Chinese Music; Mass Communications; Business Administration; and International Affairs with Cybersecurity; Harriet has always loved exploring and visiting new places. Working both in consultancies and in-house corporate roles, after nearly 30 years of desk-bound life, she changed her lifestyle to set up her own communications consultancy, creating greater flexibility to enjoy trail-running and participate in trail races. As one of the few foreigners attending races in China, Harriet started writing to share her experiences and encourage others to join. In addition to writing about trail-running, Harriet also writes about business topics such as AI and ethics and is a regular speaker on public relations-related topics.

For the latest stories and updates:

Instagram: trailingaroundasia

Web: www.trailingaroundasia.com

E-mail: info@trailingaroundasia.com

Printed in Great Britain
by Amazon

59184570R00046